TOP▷REQUESTED Standards SHEET MUSIC

0 GREAT AMERICAN SONGBOOK AND JAZZ FAVORITES

Contents

Produced by
Alfred Music Publishing Co., Inc.
P.O. Box 10003
Van Nuys, CA 91410-0003
alfred.com

Printed in USA.

ISBN-10: 0-7390-9419-X
ISBN-13: 978-0-7390-9419-8
Cover photo: © Shutterstock / Andrii Muzyka

AIN'T MISBEHAVIN'

Words by
ANDY RAZAF

Music by
THOMAS "FATS" WALLER and HARRY BROOKS

6

the one I love.   I'm thru with flirt-in',   it's   just you I'm think-in' of.

Ain't mis-be-hav-in',   I'm sav-in' my love for   you._____

_____   Like Jack Hor-ner   in the cor-ner,

don't go no-where;   what do I care.   Your kiss-es

AT LAST

Lyrics by
MACK GORDON

Music by
HARRY WARREN

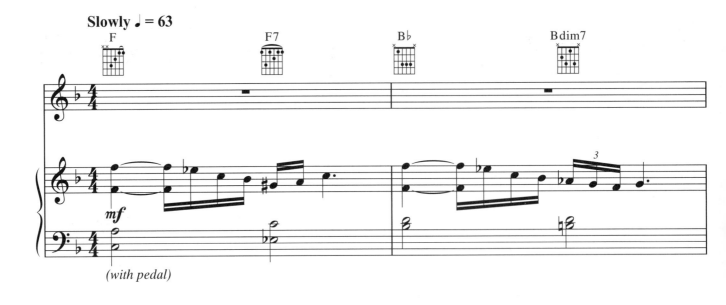

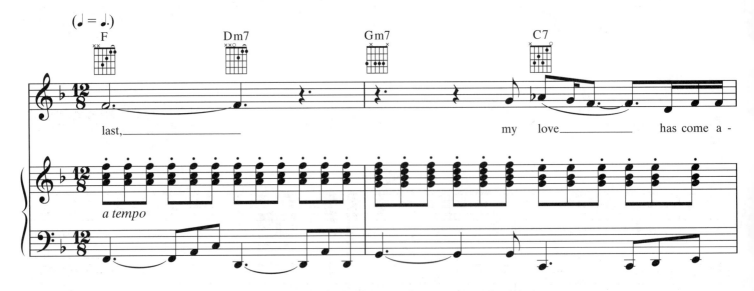

At Last - 5 - 1

10

BLUE MOON

Lyrics by
LORENZ HART

Music by
RICHARD RODGERS

Blue Moon - 3 - 1

DON'T GET AROUND MUCH ANYMORE

Lyrics by
BOB RUSSELL

Music by
DUKE ELLINGTON

Don't Get Around Much Anymore - 4 - 1

DON'T SIT UNDER THE APPLE TREE
(With Anyone Else But Me)

1 full verse

Words and Music by
CHARLIE TOBIAS, LEW BROWN
and SAM H. STEPT

2/2
Bb

Don't Sit Under the Apple Tree - 5 - 1

(see additional lyric)

I come march-ing home._____ I
I

just got word from the guy who heard from the guy next door to
told the gang, the whole she-bang, that you were sweet and

me, the girl he met just loves to pet and it
true, they ran right out and came right back with a

fits you to a 'T.' So! Don't sit un-der the ap-ple tree with
pho-to-graph of you.

24

Though navy blue may appeal to you when you meet a bold Jack Tar
Don't be a sport when the fleet's in port 'cos you know what sailors are. So!

Be dumb and deaf when the R.A.F. say 'The moon is shining bright!'
They might take sips from your red lips as 'The target for tonight!' So!

That apple tree knows the history of our meetings after dark
I'd hate to find other names entwined with yours, upon the bark. So!

You sat with me 'neath the apple tree when I stole our first love kiss
I won't deny Ma's apple pie ain't the only thing I miss. So!

I PUT A SPELL ON YOU

Words and Music by
JAY HAKWINS

I'M IN THE MOOD FOR LOVE

Words and Music by
JIMMY McHUGH and DOROTHY FIELDS

I'm in the mood for love, sim-ply be-cause you're near me, fun-ny, but when you're near me, I'm in the mood for love.

I'm in the Mood for Love - 3 - 1

LAURA

Lyrics by
JOHNNY MERCER

Music by
DAVID RAKSIN

Lau - ra___ is the face in the mist - y light,___ foot - steps___

___ that you hear down the hall.___ The laugh

Laura - 3 - 1

32

Laura - 3 - 3

MOONLIGHT SERENADE

Lyrics by
MITCHELL PARISH

Music by
GLENN MILLER

Moonlight Serenade - 3 - 1

stars_____ are a - glow_____ and to - night,___ how their light___ sets me dream-ing. My

love,_____ do you know_____ that your eyes___ are like stars___ bright-ly beam-ing? I

bring you and sing you a moon - light ser - e - nade.

Let us stray 'til break of day in love's val - ley of dreams. Just

MY MAN

Words by
ALBERT WILLEMETZ and JACQUES CHARLES
English Lyric by
CHANNING POLLOCK

Music by
MAURICE YVAIN

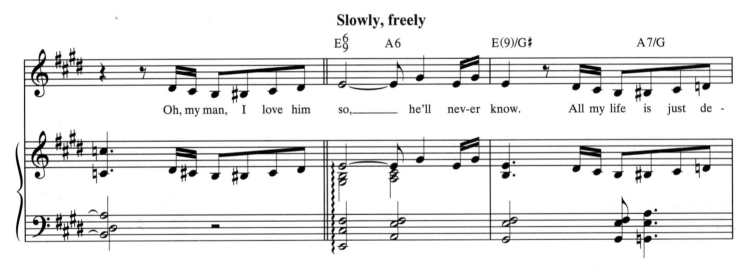

Oh, my man, I love him so,____ he'll nev-er know. All my life is just de-

spair, but I don't care. When he takes me in his

My Man - 5 - 1

42

THEME FROM "NEW YORK, NEW YORK"

Words by
FRED EBB

Music by
JOHN KANDER

Theme From "New York, New York" - 5 - 1

46

Verse 2:

ORANGE COLORED SKY

Words and Music by
MILTON DELUGG and
WILLIE STEIN

I was walk-in' a-long__ mind-in' my bus-'ness when

out of an or-ange col-ored sky, Flash! Bam!

Chorus: (Wistfully)

Violent

(crash) *(crash)*

Orange Colored Sky - 4 - 1

OVER THE RAINBOW
(from *The Wizard of Oz*)

Lyrics by
E.Y. HARBURG

Music by
HAROLD ARLEN

Over the Rainbow - 3 - 1

56

Over the Rainbow - 3 - 3

WHATEVER LOLA WANTS

(from *Damn Yankees*)

(Cue:) **LOLA:** And do like Lola tells you to do.

Words and Music by
RICHARD ADLER and JERRY ROSS

Whatever Lola Wants - 3 - 1

58

59

Whatever Lola Wants - 3 - 3

THE PINK PANTHER

By HENRY MANCINI

THE SHADOW OF YOUR SMILE

Lyric by
PAUL FRANCIS WEBSTER

Music by
JOHNNY MANDEL

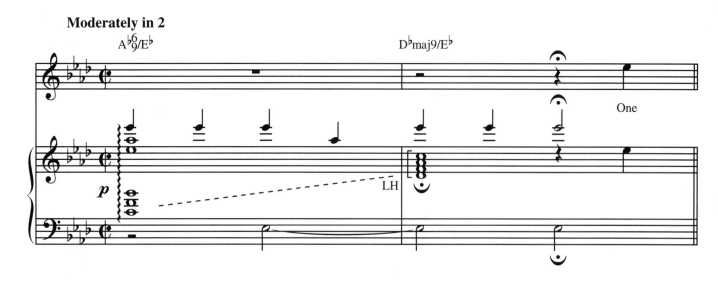

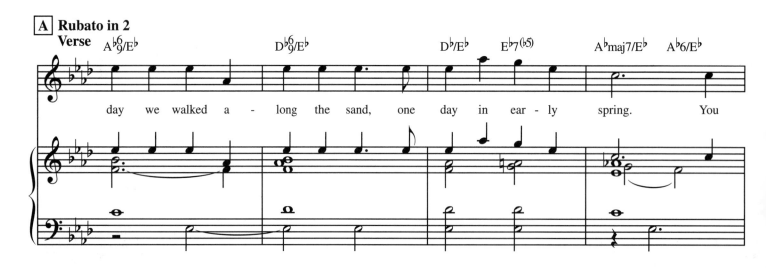

day we walked a - long the sand, one day in ear - ly spring. You

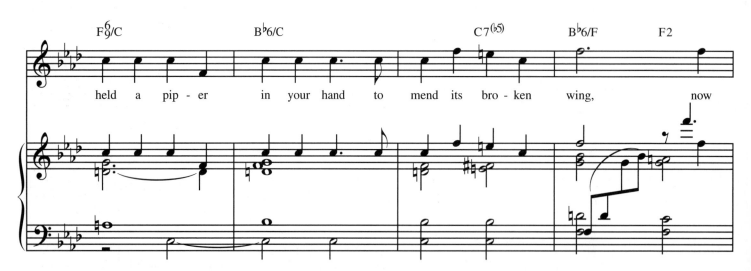

held a pip - er in your hand to mend its bro - ken wing, now

The Shadow of Your Smile - 4 - 1

STRAIGHTEN UP AND FLY RIGHT

Words and Music by
NAT "KING" COLE and IRVING MILLS

TAKE FIVE

By PAUL DESMOND

74

WHAT A WONDERFUL WORLD

Words and Music by
GEORGE DAVID WEISS and BOB THIELE

What a Wonderful World - 4 - 1